Books by William Meredith

Translated by William Meredith

Edited by William Meredith

Other Poems

WILLIAM MEREDITH was born in New York City in 1919, was graduated from Princeton in 1940, and served as a naval aviator during the war. His first book of poems, *Love Letter from an Impossible Land*, was chosen by Archibald MacLeish, in 1944, for the Yale Series of Younger Poets; the title poem was written the year before, in the Aleutian Islands. *Ships and Other Figures*, his second book of verse, was published in Princeton in 1948, and *The Open Sea*, his third, by Knopf in 1958.

William Meredith has won three of *Poetry*'s annual prizes, a grant from the National Academy of Arts and Letters, and one from the Ford Foundation to study opera; he was recently elected a chancellor of the Academy of American Poets. Mr. Meredith has taught at Princeton, at the University of Hawaii, at Middlebury, Breadloaf, and for the past seven years at Connecticut College.

The Wreck of the Thresher

and Other Poems

by William Meredith

NEW YORK: ALFRED A. KNOPF 1964

ACKNOWLEDGMENTS

"Autumn Crocuses" © 1964 by Shenandoah. Reprinted from *Shenandoah*, Winter Issue.

"Rhenish Night" © 1964 by The United Chapters of Phi Beta Kappa. Reprinted from *The American Scholar*, Vol. XXXIII, No. 2, Spring, 1964.

"For His Father," "Roots," and "Iambic Feet Considered as Honorable Scars" appeared originally in *Poetry*.

"An Old Field Mowed" (now titled "An Old Field Mowed for Appearances' Sake") and "Guillaume Apollinaire" (now titled "For Guillaume Apollinaire") appeared originally in *The New Yorker*.

Most of the other poems in this volume first appeared in *The Hudson Review*, *Princeton Library Chronicle*, *Partisan Review*, *Voices*, *The New York Review of Books*, *The Wisconsin Studies in Contemporary Literature*, *The Virginia Quarterly Review*, *The Paris Review*, and a souvenir program for The New York City Ballet.

L. C. catalog card number: 64-14418

This is a BORZOI BOOK, *published by* ALFRED A. KNOPF, INC.

FIRST EDITION

for Robert Drew

Contents

The Wreck of the Thresher and Other Poems

The Wreck of the Thresher *(Lost at sea, April 10, 1963)*

I stand on the ledge where rock runs into the river
As the night turns brackish with morning, and mourn the
    drowned.
Here the sea is diluted with river; I watch it slaver
Like a dog curing of rabies. Its ravening over,
Lickspittle ocean nuzzles the dry ground.
(But the dream that woke me was worse than the sea's gray
Slip-slap; there are no such sounds by day.)

This crushing of people is something we live with.
Daily, by unaccountable whim
Or caught up in some harebrained scheme of death,
Tangled in cars, dropped from the sky, in flame,
Men and women break the pledge of breath:
And now under water, gone all jetsam and small
In the pressure of oceans collected, a squad of brave men in a hull.

(Why can't our dreams be content with the terrible facts?
The only animal cursed with responsible sleep,
We trace disaster always to our own acts.
I met a monstrous self trapped in the black deep:
All these years, he smiled, *I've drilled at sea*
For this crush of water. Then he saved only me.)

3

We invest ships with life. Look at a harbor
At first light: with better grace than men
In their movements the vessels run to their labors
Working the fields that the tide has made green again;
Their beauty is womanly, they are named for ladies and queens,
Although by a wise superstition these are called
After fish, the finned boats, silent and submarine.
The crushing of any ship has always been held
In dread, like a house burned or a great tree felled.

I think of how sailors laugh, as if cold and wet
And dark and lost were their private, funny derision
And I can judge then what dark compression
Astonishes them now, their sunken faces set
Unsmiling, where the currents sluice to and fro
And without humor, somewhere northeast of here and below.

(*Sea-brothers, I lower you the ingenuity of dreams,*
Strange lungs and bells to escape in; let me stay aboard last—
We amend our dreams in half-sleep. Then it seems
Easy to talk to the severe dead and explain the past.
Now they are saying, *Do not be ashamed to stay alive,*
You have dreamt nothing that we do not forgive.
And gentlier, *Study something deeper than yourselves,*
As, how the heart, when it turns diver, delves and saves.)

4

Whether we give assent to this or rage
Is a question of temperament and does not matter.
Some will has been done past our understanding,
Past our guilt surely, equal to our fears.
Dullards, we are set again to the cryptic blank page
Where the sea schools us with terrible water.
The noise of a boat breaking up and its men is in our ears.
The bottom here is too far down for our sounding;
The ocean was salt before we crawled to tears.

Orpheus
for Franklin and Helen Reeve

The lute and my skill with it came unasked from Apollo,
But the girl I drew myself from the trunk of a tree
And she lodged in me then as she had in the black willow.
I was tuned like strings: she had the skill of me.

She was taken by death on one of three pretenses:
A jealous brother, a jealous god, or a serpent.
The mind turns from causes in such cases—
All a man can say is, it happened.

Now with my father's favors, the lute and skill,
Through the dark smelly places where the gods play
With the unlucky, I ape a smiling way
And do prodigious feats of vaudeville.

The meaningless ordeals I've tuned to reason!
The foul caprice I've zithered into just!
As if my love were no more than a god's lust,
Lend me Euridice, I sing and sing.

On Falling Asleep to Birdsong

In a tree at the edge of the clearing
A whippoorwill calls in the dark,
An American forest bird.
Lying in bed I hear him;
He is old, or at least no answer
Comes from the wood behind him;
I lose him there in the topmost
Invisible twigs in my head.

At the edge of the town I grow old
On a farm, sooner or later.
Lying alone at night
I remember my father and mother;
I see them, not tossing together
In their concern over me
But propped on separate pillows,
Going away like trees
A leaf at a time and angry
At the wingless, terrible trip;
And asking if they can stay.

I thrash in bed at forty
Reluctant to go on that trip.
I conjure nightingales
With their lovely lecherous song—
This is a question of will
And I conjure those silky birds

Tossing the boughs like bedsprings,
Fluting themselves to death
In music that will not cool.
Ah, I like it better
With the randy foreign fowl
When summer had her fill.
But I am in bed in the fall
And cannot arrest the dream
That unwinds a chase and a rape
And ends in Tracian pain.

Although no bird comes,
The whippoorwill does not mourn.
At the bourn of human farms
He holds a constant song;
When time has gone away
He calls to what he calls.
Dark bird, we will prevail
If life indeed is one—
The fluting time and now,
Now and the pillow-time
Propped with knowledge and pain.
If some dark call repeats
And means the same and more,
The rest I will endure.
If it is one, dark bird

Who watch my middle sleep,
I will grow old, as a man
Will read of a transformation:
Knowing it is a fable
Contrived to answer a question
Answered, if ever, in fables,
Yet all of a piece and clever
And at some level, true.

For His Father

When I was young I looked high and low for a father,
And what blond sons you must have tried on then!
But only your blood could give us our two men
And in the end we settled for one another.

Whatever death is, it sets pretenders free.
The secret loss or boy or self-defense
That won me your affectionate pretense
Is in a grave. Now you judge only me.

But like a living son I go on railing
A little, or praising under my breath,
Not knowing the generosity of death,
Fearing your judgment on my old failing.

Dear ghost, take pleasure in our good report,
And bully me no further with my blame.
You use my eyes at last; I sign your name
Deliberately beneath my life and art.

Roots

Mrs. Leamington stood on a cloud,
Quarreling with a dragon—it was May,
When things tend to look allegorical—
As I drove up the hill that silhouettes
Her house against the east. In any month
She's hard to place—scattered and sibylline:
She hangs the curtains for me in the fall
(Rather than let me ruin them myself)
And warns me about thieves and moths and women—
Nothing for money, all for neighborhood.

'My god you get out early, Mrs. L,'
I said to her. 'I don't sleep well,' she said,
'Everybody drinks too much today.
Where this root's tree is, I'll never know.'
I joined her like a knight in his good clothes
And we rode the hairy serpent through the grass
To the edge of the rectangle she was turning up,
But he was saying nothing, by his depth
Or diameter, about which way he'd come from.
There was a row of planted Norway maple
Along the drive, a hundred feet away,
But this yellow runner didn't look like them.
I cut it with the spade and smelled its tail.
'Nothing I could recognize,' she said.
'There's some new aspen skittering in the wood
Behind the house. I'll bet it comes from them.'

She chopped at what was left with a short hoe.
'It's roots I'm putting in, as a matter of fact—
Fat and tidy little roots, potatoes.
There's no room for them in the kitchen garden
But someone sent me special ones this year
From Canada. Let's go and get some coffee.'

Dishtowels and her nylon underwear
Were on the clothes tree; straining at the door
Was her Mercedes. It was half past eight.
We sat in the kitchen on her good antiques.
'Have you ever really thought about the roots,'
She asked, filling a pair of luster cups,
'What a world they are, swaying in the thick air
Under us, upside down?'
                                    I'd thought about them
All the week before, when the elms were budding,
The twigs so delicate we might have had
A Chinese landscapist for first selectman
Who put out all the town roads to wild plum.
In a week they would be plain leafy elms—
Not a gross thing to be, god knows, but coarser—
And I'd thought how their roots all year around
Would keep that primavera delicacy.
So I said, 'I have, a little. What about them?'

'When I was a girl, my father put those cedars
In the hedge along the road. He told us then
(I don't suppose it's true but it ought to be)
That a tree repeats its structure, up and down,
The roots mirroring the branches; and he showed
Us how the tap-root of a cedar tree
Is the same length as the trunk, and the green brush
In the air is shaped like the brown brush in the earth.
Did you ever notice the trees in Fragonard?'

'They don't look real,' I said, 'They look like coral.'

'They look like roots, is what they look like. Wait.'
She went and got a book of reproductions
And showed me the lady swinging on the swing
In a mass of greenery and silk and cloud.
Then suddenly she turned it upside down
And the cloudy leaves and the clouds turned into rocks
And the boles of the trees were gripping them like rocks.
'Think of the branches tossing in the loam,
Reaching for rays of water, the way leaves
Arrange themselves for sunlight, except lacier.'

'Does Pluto keep potatoes in a vase
Like zinnias, do you suppose?' I asked.

Her face took on the aspect of quotation.
' "The Magus Zoroaster, my dead child,"
—That's Shelley, the Spirit of Earth in Shelley—
"Met his own image walking in the garden.
That apparition, sole of men, he saw.
For know there are two worlds of life and death:
One that which thou beholdest; but the other
Is underneath the grave, where do inhabit
The shadows of all forms that think and live,
Till death unite them and they part no more."
—Prometheus Unbound, a long dull poem.
Please use the ashtray, not my luster saucer.'

'The strangest thing would be to meet yourself.
Above ground or below I wouldn't like it.'

The gothic-blossomed tree of Leamingtons,
Her husband's run-out people in the south
(He sleeps in Arlington in Captain's stripes)
Seemed to catch but didn't hold her eye.
'I've been thinking about dying,' she went on.

'I'll be seventy-four this summer, so I ought to.
Some of my mother's people are right here,
On this place, I mean, just across the road.
It used to be a graveyard. There are beech trees
All around it and a view up-river.
Maybe I'll have them put me there intact;
I used to say I'd like to drift as ashes
Over the fields, and give them that much back.
But more and more I think of the beech roots
Holding up stones like blossoms or like nests
Or like the colored stones on a jade tree—
That slope was never cleared, it's mostly stones—
And in the lower branches, a tree-house:
A box in the ground where I meet my own image sleeping,
The soft brown branches raising it aloft—
Except aloft is down or I sleep face down.
Well, back to my spuds, she said. Don't you hate that word?
Yet it's good middle English. Stop on your way home.
By then perhaps we'll both have earned a drink.'

Two Japanese Maples

How can the snow,
Come all that way,
Remember to stay
In the twigs of these
Two delicate trees
In tufts just so
And be Japanese
And yet still know
With the dogwood and spruce
To flurry and play
As fast & loose
As the U.S.A.?

An Old Field Mowed for Appearances' Sake

My loud machine for making hay
Mutters about our work today;
Through bushes and small trees it flails—
Blueberry, sumac, cherry, bay.

I lay the little woods in swales
To burn them as the daylight fails
For no surviving horse or cow
Is fed such crazy salad bales.

They fall like jackstraws, anyhow,
Or like the forest, trunk and bough
That harder hands and will than these
Burned once, where it is meadow now.

I side with meadow against trees
Because of woodsmoke in the breeze,
The ghost of other foes—though both
Would find us puny enemies,
Second growth and second growth.

On Looking into Robert Frost in Kanji*

Poetry can be defined as what is lost in translation.
ROBERT FROST

There are more problems to a woodchuck
Than the old tongue-twister dreamed.
How much of the *wood* is picture,
How much idea or noise?
Could an oriental nature-lover know
The restless action of the verb *to chuck*?
Will the nice mixture of Virgil and Vermont
Find an equivalent voice
On the spare Japanese reed?

After what might be described locally
As seven elegant hen-tracks
The translator remarks
Very sensibly: (*woodchuck*)
As if to paraphrase his unyielding poet:
The definition of woodchuck is,
That which is lost in translation.

*Kanji: The characters used in printing Japanese.

18

An Assent to Wildflowers

"Ay" and "no" too was no good divinity.
KING LEAR

Plucked from their sockets like eyes that gave offense,
Dozens of black-eyed susans gaze
Into the room—a composite lens
Like a fly's, staring out of a bronze vase.

Gloucestered out of the meadow by the hands
I love, they ask me do I know
What they mean by this bold flower-glance?
Do I know who made the room glow?

And the answer of course is love, but before I can say
Love, I see the other question they raise,
Like anything blind that gapes at you that way.
A man may see how this world goes with no eyes.

The luster of the room goes blear for a minute,
Then, like Gloucester, I begin to guess.
I imagine the world, I imagine the world and you in it:
There's flowering, there's a dark question answered yes.

For Guillaume Apollinaire

The day is colorless like Swiss characters in a novel
And I sit at a desk in an old house left to the arts
Teaching your poems English.
I have read the French words in the dictionary starting
     with "W."
They are borrowings, too: *wesleyen, wigwam, wisigoth*
And *wattman,* an archaic electrical-tram driver.
If you were alive this summer you'd be 82.

The fourth floor of the mansion, just less than an acre,
Is servants' country. For years it was settled—
Chambermaids, kitchenmaids, footmen, a butler, a cook.
Somewhere there must be almost an acre of them now
Laid out in the Romanesque floor plan under the sod,
And the lady who rang for them.
The house is a good place to work. But these poems—
How quickly the strangeness would pass from things
     if it were not for them.

Five Poems of Guillaume Apollinaire (*translations*)

I

AUTUMN CROCUSES

In fall the fields are poisonous but fair
Where, slowly poisoning, the cattle graze.
The meadow saffron, *colchicum*, thrives there,
Color of lilac and the circles under eyes.
My life pastures so on the autumn hue
Of your eyes and slowly poisons itself too.
Children in queer jackets come and play
Harmonicas and pick the purple flowers
Which are like mothers, their own daughters' daughters.
When your saffron eyelids raise and lower
They are like flowers that a crazy wind flutters.
The shepherd sings the cattle on their way
As, slow and lowingly and for all time, they pass
From the broad evil-flowered autumn grass.

II
ANNIE

Between Mobile and Galveston
On the seacoast of Texas
There's a big garden full of rosebushes
And a house like a big rose.

Often there is a woman
Walking alone in the garden
And when I pass on the lime-bordered highway
We look at one another.

She is a Mennonite, this woman,
And her rosebushes and her clothes are buttonless.
I see that two buttons are missing from my jacket.
The lady and I observe almost the same rite.

III
MOUNTEBANKS

The mountebanks appear like smoke
And through the churchless village walk
Passing the door of the gray inn
And off like smoke across the plain.

The children run in front and mime
Their elders follow in a dream
Fruit trees resign themselves to pillage
Once this music wakes the village.

They carry odd-shaped weights and props
And thumping drums and gilded hoops
And beasts with cups interpret where
They pass, a monkey and a bear.

IV
AUTUMN

In the fog a farmer with a hobbled leg
And his ox pass slowly by, in the autumn fog
That hides the villages, beggared and dumb;
And as he passes you hear the farmer hum
A song about love and a lover forsaken,
It tells of a ring and a heart that gets broken.
Oh, autumn, autumn has made summer die.
In the fog two gray silhouettes pass by.

V

RHENISH NIGHT

My glass is filled with a wine that trembles like flame.
Listen, a boatman is singing a slow song
About a moonlight night when seven women came
Out of the river and their hair was green and long.

Now sing and dance until the terrace whirls
And the boatman's slow song fades
And bring me all the pretty blond-haired girls
With the still gaze and the coiled braids.

The Rhine flows drunk, its vine-leaves trailing after,
The trembling gold of night is mirrored there.
Like a death-rattle the slow song grows softer
About the nymphs who bewitched the summer with
     their green hair—

My glass has shattered like a peal of laughter.

Fables about Error

i: *A Ritual Mouse*

The mouse in the cupboard repeats himself.
Every morning he lies upside down
Astonished at the violence of the spring
That has tumbled him and the flimsy trap again.
His beady expressionless eyes do not speak
Of the terrible moment we sleep through.
Sometimes a little blood runs from his mouth,
Small and dry like his person.
I throw him into the laurel bush as being too small
To give the offenses that occasion burial.

It begins to be winter; he is a field mouse
And comes in, but how unwisely, from the cold.
Elsewhere now, and from their own points of view,
Cats and poisoners are making the same criticism:
He seems no wiser for having been taken
A dozen nights running. He looks weak;
Given a subtler trap he might have informed
Or tried to bargain with whatever it is mice have.

Surely there is always that in experience
Which could warn us; and the worst
That can be said of any of us is:
He did not pay attention.

ii: *A Fable of Grackles*

Like a rift of acrid smoke
A flock of grackles fling in from the river
And fight for the winter sun
Or for seed, is it, in the flailed grass.
Their speech is a mean and endless quarrel
And even in their rising
They keep a sense of strife, flat across the orchard;
Viciousness and greed
Sharpen the spaces of sky between them.

Tonight will bring the dream of fire in the theater
Where rancour drifts through the building
And at the exit, where the screaming should be,
We will trample each other in silence,
And no one get to safety
And no one yield in love.

iii: *The Tale of the House Swallow on Cape Ann*
(alluding to *The Symposium* of Plato)

A fluttering bird in the first soft heat of June,
She clung to the feathery elm, swinging and swinging,
Inviting a mate from the Massachusetts air.
(Each of us then is but the tally of a creature,
Plato's Aristophanes had said.)

But more than one mate came; they filled the warm sky
With dispute of her. For a long, fluttering while
She swayed in the tree-top, alone, swaying.
(The body is always looking for its other,
He said, though it is not bodies alone that mate.)

What she did next made the whole party laugh.
Wanton, we called her, and husbands and wives took hands:
She was followed by four males into the dark birdhouse.
(In the dark we would solve impulsively the riddle
That even civilized Plato did not get right.)

There was no quarreling in the birdhouse then.
We went in to dinner. Who hatched those eggs
With her, fed and fledged those little swallows,
Aristophanes? Ah, he replies, the ghosting spirit
Is another, more jagged shape. This puzzle is not of flesh;

Many people in Massachusetts are moved by lust,
Their hearts yearn for unseemly fittings-together
Which their minds disown. Man is aflutter
For the beautiful, Diotima told Socrates,
But the flesh is no more than an instance for the mind
    to consider.

iv: *Moral*

W hat is as wrong as the uninstructed heart?
Left to its ends, it clutches things and creatures
That can't be held, or held, will slip their natures;
It lives to hoard or to protect a hoard.
To school, to school! Teach the poor organ skill
That all its ignorant, nervous will
Does not unpage us like old calendars.
A life should be all gathering and art.

Let there be academies of everything,
That the trap in the warm kitchen yield to guile,
That grackles leave a fire single file
And swallows find their true halves the first spring.
The mind should be, like art, a gathering
Where the red heart that fumes in the chest
Saying *kill, kill, kill* or *love, love, love,*
Gentled of the need to be possessed,
Can study a little the things that it dreams of.

(*Phi Beta Kappa poem read at Columbia University
June 1, 1959*)

The Couple Overhead

They don't get anywhere,
The couple overhead;
They wrangle like the damned
In the bed above my bed,
But the harm has all been done.
And this is a short despair:
Count Ugolino dead
Was endlessly condemned
To gnaw the archbishop's head
Where the nape and the skull are one.

Not so, these secular drunks.
Dante would find their treason
Too spiritless to keep;
Like children stealing raisins
They eat each other's eyes;
The ice that grips their flanks
Is something they have frozen.
After a while they sleep;
And the punishment they've chosen,
After a while it dies.

At the Opera

This queen, caught up in error,
Who cries so sweetly out
Against her own hard laws,
Might put all grief in doubt
By her repetitious furor,
Her rallies to applause.

But no one minds her sawing
The air and looking perfectly unreal,
Or remembers what he's *seen*
In the foolhardy ordeal
We are brought through by her being
Every decibel a queen.

Dialogue at the Ballet

What brings *you* to the cages of beauty?
Bodies or limbs or faces
Or do you hope to learn more grace than you knew before?
But your body is too thick-tongued to talk to these.

I learn: the passage of even myself through space
Ought to be as courteous as a planet's duty;
And the heavy man I brought in through the door
Goes out heavy, but at dancer's ease.

The Ballet

In a cage of light, the splendid creatures
With faces amenable to anything,
Doing whatever you like—fountains
Of work or cascades of pretty failure.
With flanks as clean as bone they signal one another
On the far side of a trench of music—
Such breasts and hair, such bold genitals

Until you would think we were the caged ones
Where our bodies shift and mumble
In the dark-tunneled house,
Waiting for feeding-time and after that, sleep;
We watch the loping things from the zoo of ourselves.

Yet it is not only their perfection detains
Us in the paunchy dark, it is pity too.
That they must signal that way, like eloquent mutes?
Yes, and a longer affliction of splendor:
That it cannot reproduce its kind.

Five Accounts of a Monogamous Man

i: *He thinks of the Chinese snake who is*
the beginning and the end

If you or I should die
That day desire would not renew
Itself in any bed.
The old snake of the world, eternity
That holds his tail in his mouth,
Would spit it out
And ease off through the grass
Like a piece of music
To we don't know where.

Then it would be for the living
To beat the grass and bring him back.
But would he be set tamely
To sucking his tail again
In that absence?

ii: *He marvels at the persistence of passion*

Like black duennas the hours sit
And read our lips and watch our thighs.
The years are pederasts: they wait
For boys and will not meet my eyes.

And children are cool astronomers
Who scan us like old galaxies
And calculate how many years
Before we'll turn to gas or freeze.

And yet sometimes I have to shave
And brush my teeth at dawn to keep
My healthy middle-aged alive
Hands off you where you lie asleep.

iii: *Sometimes he contemplates adultery*

I had no insanity to excuse this,
But for a week my heart ran with another love,
Imagined another house, down to its books and bed.
My miserable fluttered heart, you understand, chose this.
Now I am led home—cold, grave,
Contractual as a dog—by my scurrilous head.

iv: *His hands, on a trip to Wisconsin*

It is night. I am a thousand miles from home.
My hands lie awake and are aware of themselves,
One on my noisy chest, the other, the right one,
A matter of several pounds, oppressing my forehead.
It is a week since it fluted the air goodbye.
I think of the path in space the thing has made,
Veering and halting; of the shapes hands make
Washing a car, or in the uses of music.

Two shapes it has traced honor this right hand:
The curve that a plane rides out
As it leaves or takes a deck on the scalloped sea;
Handily, handily then this two-pound creature
Felt the wired air, let the two monsters kiss.
The shapes that it graphed were fairer
Than the hair of the clouds that watched
Or the sea's own scalloped hair.

And he and his gauche fellow, moving symmetrically,
Have described one body so well
They could dress that shape in air
As they long to do now though they lie
Laced hunks of flesh on my belly—
Ahead of them some years of roving
Before the white landscape of age checks them,

Your body's disaster, sure to be traced there,
Even so slight a change in a dear shape
Halting them, baffled, lascivious suddenly,
Or folded cold, or feeling your hands folded cold.

v: *Lines from his guest-book*

Shelley's houses and walks were always a clutter of women,
And god knows what further arrangements he kept in his mind.
Drôle de ménage, Rimbaud said of himself and Verlaine,
As if there were any other kind.
In Yeats' tower, in all that fakery of ghosts,
Some solid women came and slept as Mrs. Yeats' guests.
We are most our own strange selves when we are hosts.

Here those who have loved or befriended me come to a proof:
They must lodge in my head and in company under one roof.
Keeping house is the instinct of love; it is always
        a little ridiculous.
Yet it is with no light welcome I welcome the friends of the
        house.

About Poetry

i: *The Poet as Troublemaker*

She likes to split an apple down the middle
And with her hands behind her ask them, which?
The other children fall in with the riddle
But he says, both hands! both hands, you sly old bitch!

ii: *Iambic Feet Considered as Honorable Scars*

You see these little scars? That's where my wife
—The principle of order everywhere—
Has grazed me, shooting at the sloppy bear
That lurches from the urinals of life.
He is the principle of god knows what;
He wants things to be shapeless and all hair.
Only a fool would want to fight him fair,
Only a woman would think he could be shot.

Drawing the Face

i: *Self-portrait*

If these years keep making up
Like the pellets of old stars
Or the hail from comets' tails
That pocks the fields of space;
If liquor and business and love
And the seasons don't let up soon,
My god, I'll die with a marvelous face,
Cratered and used like the moon.

ii: *A Young Girl Reading* The Poetics

It follows that we must draw men
Either as better than in real life,
Or as worse, or as they are."
Look, Time is wrinkling his wife:
A smooth-browed girl reading Aristotle,
Her notebook open and white,
And as much to the years as the girl
I say, write.

The Preponderance

To me there appears an immense preponderance of virtue and happiness even in this world, wicked and miserable as it is represented.

JOHN ADAMS

Headless fountains
running loose,
I've killed some chickens
I've seen a goose
I've thought of people
cut up for soap
but there's more to this
than chicken hope
or the chicken scare
that sells what's dear.

I read, I love
I eat, I drink
I watch the world tilt
I watch the children think:
there's so much to it
and most of it good
that while I've tendons
to lift my head,
like a rooster drinking
I'll nod to God
and save despair
for when I'm dead.

To Bertolt Brecht

I've heard that you said, when a scene you had revised
Still didn't suit a man you used to know,
"But I am not Kafka!" What artist hasn't sized
Himself in the dwindling lacquer row
Of chinese dolls that, with no loss of face,
Can be put back inside one another now
And only a fool quarrel about his place.

There are such ranks; and yet I quarrel with
Those who have put a price on mere despair,
Ranking a man as he can fetch up death
And senselessness, and finding you famous so.
You called your foe by name, a naïve faith.
It is a naïve disillusion, everywhere
Fudging the good and bad, that we must call foe.

The truth is hidden as cunningly from one
Time as another; what they change is the decoys,
And it takes a wily man to use the gun.
I think you would not be fooled by our bully-boys
Who said, "As Brecht said, I live in an age of blood."
You might stop with an oath their shrill, untimely noise:
Evil is nothing until it touches good.

An Old Photograph of Strangers

On the big staircase in this picture
They are having a pageant.
The queen comes down between heralds whose trumpets are raised
And a man, also in fancy dress, welcomes the queen
And there is another woman in powdered hair
At the foot of the staircase, acting.
The rest of the people are guests
But caught up in the moment and serious,
In evening clothes of the nineties,
They look only slightly more real.
I suppose they are all dead now
But some of their faces are just like faces today.

It seems to be lighted electrically
Or by very bright gaslight, behind us.
They must have held still a long time.
A dark young man is holding a watch that opens.
The girl whose head is too near
And that old man settling his glasses would always have blurred.

On the landing a stained-glass goddess
In milky Tiffany glass
Is faint where her window is dark. She is faint, it seems,
With the darkness outside on this one particular night.

Consequences

i: *of Choice*

Despair is big with friends I love,
Hydrogen and burning Jews.
I give them all the grief I have
But I tell them, friends, I choose, I choose,

Don't make me say against my glands
Or how the world has treated me.
Though gay and modest give offense
And people grieve pretentiously,

More than I hoped to do, I do
And more than I deserve I get;
What little I attend, I know
And it argues order more than not.

My desperate friends, I want to tell
Them, you take too delicate offense
At the stench of time and man's own smell,
It is only the smell of consequence.

Consequences

ii: *of Love*

People love each other and the light
Of love gilds but doesn't alter,
People don't change one another, can scarcely
By taking will and thought add a little
Now and then to their own statures
Which, praise them, they do,
So that here we are in all our sizes
Flooded in the impartial daylight sometimes,
Spotted sometimes in a light we make ourselves,
Human, the beams of attention
Of social animals at their work
Which is loving; and sometimes all dark.

The only correction is
By you of you, by me of me.
People are worth looking at in this light
And if you listen what they are saying is,
Love me sun out there whoever you are,
Chasing me from bed in the morning,
Spooking me all day with shadow,
Surprising me whenever you fall;
Make me conspicuous as I go here,
Spotted by however many beams,
Now light, finally dark. *I fear*
There is meant to be a lot of darkness,
You hear them say, but every last creature
Is the one it meant to be.

Consequences

iii: *My Acts*

The acts of my life swarm down the street like Puerto
    Rican kids,
Foreign but small and, except for one, unknived.
They do no harm though their voices slash like reeds;
All except one they have evidently been loved.

And down the hill where I've planted spruce and red pine
In a gang of spiked shadows they slouch at night.
I am reasonably brave. I have been, except on one occasion,
Myself: it is no good trying to be what you are not.

We live among gangs who seem to have no stake
In what we're trying to do, no sense of property or race,
Yet if you speak with authority they will halt and break
And sullenly, one by one, show you a local face.

I dreamt once that they caught me and, holding me down,
Burned my genitals with gasoline;
In my stupid terror I was telling them names
So my manhood kept and the rest went up in flames.

"Now, say the world is a fair place," the biggest one said,
And because there was no face worse than my own there
I said it and got up. Quite a lot of me is charred.
By our code it is fair. We play fair. The world is fair.

A NOTE ON THE AUTHOR

WILLIAM MEREDITH was born in New York City in 1919, was graduated from Princeton in 1940, and served as a naval aviator during the war. His first book of poems, *Love Letter from an Impossible Land*, was chosen by Archibald MacLeish, in 1944, for the Yale Series of Younger Poets; the title poem was written the year before, in the Aleutian Islands. *Ships and Other Figures*, his second book of verse, was published in Princeton in 1948, and *The Open Sea*, his third, by Knopf in 1958.

William Meredith has won three of *Poetry*'s annual prizes, a grant from the National Academy of Arts and Letters, and one from the Ford Foundation to study opera; he was recently elected a chancellor of the Academy of American Poets. Mr. Meredith has taught at Princeton, at the University of Hawaii, at Middlebury, Breadloaf, and for the past seven years at Connecticut College.

February 1964

This book was designed, composed, and printed by Clarke & Way at The Thistle Press, New York, and bound by H. Wolff, New York.

The text of the book was set on the Monotype in a type face called Walbaum, cut early in the nineteenth century by J. E. Walbaum, a type founder at Goslar and Weimar, who followed Didot in the design of this modern face. His original matrices are still in existence, and are the property of the Berthold foundry, of Berlin, Germany.